# Learn From The Failures Of Others

*Quick Guide To Entrepreneurs On Business Mistakes, How They Happen, Ways To Avoid Them, And How To Fix Them*

**Cashflow Will Kill Your Business**

Round Square Ventures Ltd

Copyright © 2019 Round Square Ventures Ltd

All rights reserved.

ISBN-13: 9781691323609

Reproduction or translation of any part of this work beyond that permitted by Section 107 or 108 of the 1976 United States Copyright Act without permission of the copyright owner is unlawful. Requests for permission or further information should be addressed to Round Square Ventures Ltd.

Please note the information contained within this document is for educational and entertainment purposes only. All effort has been executed to present accurate, up to date, and reliable, complete information. No warranties of any kind are declared or implied. Readers acknowledge that the authors are not engaging in the rendering of legal, financial, medical or professional advice. The content within this book has been derived from various sources. If legal advice or other expert assistance is required, the services of a competent professional person should be sought.

By reading this document, the reader agrees that under no circumstances are the authors responsible for any losses, direct or indirect, which are incurred as a result of the use of information contained within this document, including, but not limited to, errors, omissions, or inaccuracies.

Round Square Ventures Ltd is a company registered in England No. 07774289. Registered office: 1 Broadgate, 2nd Floor, London EC2M 2QS, United Kingdom
www.RoundSquareVentures.com
info@RoundSquareVentures.com

# RSV Business Mistakes Series

## Additional subjects in Business Mistakes Series

*Cashflow Will Kill Your Business*

*Investment Money Shouldn't Be Used For This*

*Should You Be Optimistic or Pessimistic?*

*The Plan That Will Kill Your Business*

*Sticking To The Plan Will Ruin You*

*"I'm Doing It Alone." Said No Successful Entrepreneur Ever!*

*The Staff Motivation Trap*

# CONTENTS

|   |   |   |
|---|---|---|
| | Introduction | v |
| 1 | CHAPTER I - The Mistake | 1 |
| 2 | CHAPTER II - Examples | 3 |
| 3 | CHAPTER III - How To Avoid (Start-up) | 7 |
| 4 | CHAPTER IV - How To Deal With The Problem (Established Business) | 11 |
| 5 | CHAPTER V - Summary Of Solutions | 15 |
| | About The Authors | 18 |

# INTRODUCTION

The saying goes "you learn from your mistakes". But, when it comes to being an entrepreneur, these mistakes can be very expensive and have very negative effects on your personal life and relationships.

At Round Square Ventures, we have been running small and big businesses since 1994, and we have come across so many mistakes and failures. So, we invite you to learn from our mistakes and the mistakes of others that we have witnessed over the years so that you don't have to make them yourself.

In this series, we take you down the business mistakes journey in a simple, short and very real way. In this series of these short books, we analyse the mistakes and talk about each of them in the following way:

1. **The problem:** what is it, how does it happen, and the reasons for it from both the points of view of start-ups and established businesses.
2. **Example(s):** we go through real-life examples from companies we have been involved with to bring the mistake to life and make it easier to understand. Those examples would also highlight how easy it is to fall into some traps. Whenever there may be differences between service companies and companies which sell products, we would include both examples.
3. **How start-ups can avoid it:** these are some solutions as to what we see what start-ups should do in order to avoid making those mistakes and not failing. This mainly involves talking about elements in the business planning process which need to be taken care of.
4. **How established business should deal with the problem:** in this part we are talking to an established business that has already fallen into the trap, made the mistake and needs guidance to fix things to avoid failure (if it's not too late).
5. **Summary of solutions:** we just give a brief summary of the suggested solutions for quick reference.

Make sure you look out for our other short books in this series so that you can get the full picture and avoid those potentially costly mistakes. We'd also love to hear your views and experiences in the reviews, and we're happy to answer questions. Just contact us directly on
info@roundsquareventures.com

Thanks and good luck!

Round Square Ventures Ltd

# CHAPTER I

## *The Mistake*

One of the main reasons we've seen major problems in business has been cash shortage. We consider this to be the toughest and most serious mistake and biggest reason most businesses fail. This is why we write about it first.

Some of our ventures have been very successful and profitable on paper, but the cash shortage killed them completely!

To put this into perspective, you can be selling a thousand widgets, which you have already paid for, but your customers pay you 30 days after delivery. This means that you will have to have enough cash to cover the price to buy those widgets, as well as cover all your other expenses and overheads.

Then, the problem could become even much bigger if those customers delay payment for even longer than the 30 days you were anticipating. You might start to see the problem here... The example in the next chapter should make it much clearer.

For a start-up company, the main reason for this cash shortage is usually due to a planning error involving underestimating the cash needs of the business. The plan would include the main start-up costs, some money for inventory (if you're selling products), additional work or travel not previously planned (possibly for a service business), and then not account for the delays, additional costs not previously thought about, or unforeseen expenses.

Some of the hidden costs we see in start-up planning include items such as licence fees, office deposits, insurance, website costs, utilities, transportation, and marketing. Whenever we see new entrepreneurs' business plans, we find these to be mostly underestimated. And, almost without exception, when we talk to the new entrepreneurs who write those plans, they truly believe that they won't come across those additional costs, while, also almost without exception, they face those realities within a very short period of time, even before starting operations.

For companies that sell products, underestimating cashflow needs for

# Learn From The Failures Of Others - Cashflow Will Kill Your Business

inventory and/or misplanning inventory needs are the major contributors to falling into the cash trap. The inventory cycle is usually underestimated, as well as either having cash locked into inventory which cannot be shifted or not having enough cash to fulfil new orders.

In an established business, the reasons may be somewhat similar, in that there may be some underestimation of cash needs when looking at expanding the business, but two other reasons we see leading to the eventual cash shortage are the inability to keep up with financing growing demand and overspending when the company has extra cash on hand.

We talk about underestimating cash needs and overspending in more detail in some other parts of this series, but we cover them briefly here. We talk in the next chapters in more detail about the problem of late paying customers, and ways to avoid it and how to deal with it if it becomes a problem.

It is a really tricky issue, and, of course, depending on your relationship with your customer, the potential for future business growth with them, and the reasons behind them not paying on time are all factors that make it difficult to take more aggressive steps to get paid.

# CHAPTER II

## *Examples*

We provide two real-life examples of companies which have faced the cash challenges; one selling products and the other selling services.

### *XY Company (selling products)*

One of our companies which sells products in bulk (let's call it XY) had one of its largest customers owe significant amounts, which were several months late. This happened in the following way:

1. XY made a deal with the customer to sell products in their stores, then XY gets paid 45 days after the end of each month. So, for example, all January sales will be paid mid March, February sales will be paid mid April, etc.

2. XY delivered the necessary stock to the customer for January, February and March. This stock had to be financed by XY completely, since there was no revenue yet from the customer.

3. When mid March arrived and first payment was due, the customer had issues with staff changes, and no one was available to sort out payments for XY. By the beginning of April, there was a new team to take care of the payments and they had a large backlog of similar delays with all their suppliers.

4. XY delivered necessary stock for April, still not having been paid, bringing total financing burden to 4 month, already one more month than previously anticipated. All the while, XY had to pay all overheads, as well as other expenses involved in growing the business, etc.

5. During April, the new customer team were unable to make full payments to all their suppliers, not because they didn't have the money to do it, but due to them being overwhelmed with the task, as well as new processes from the parent company involving longer payment processes and new procedures. This went on until May, and XY delivered the May stock as previously planned, bringing now the total to 5 months of inventory pre-financed and overheads and other expenses to go with it.

6. When the delays in payment continued, XY exhausted all the cash in the company, had to take a bank loan, increase their overdraft and use credit cards to cover their expenses as well as finance the additional inventory for the customer, in addition to delaying payments to their own suppliers. Moreover, the company started to get new customers who needed more inventory to be sent to them, which meant further cash strain on the company.

7. XY stopped delivering stock to the customer as they waited for payment to come. Since the customer accounted for over 70% of XY's sales, not delivering stock meant that sales went down by nearly half (since there was some stock left at the customer's shops).

As you can see, while on paper XY made a lot of sales for 6 months and looked like it was profitable, the company was on the verge of bankruptcy due to the lack of cash! The company owed a lot of money to the banks, was late paying basic overheads such as rent and utilities, delayed paying salaries, and even delayed payments to suppliers who trusted them!

The dilemma here for XY was how to approach dealing with the customer, and how the company will continue into the future (if at all possible). Business was booming, the opportunity was right there and very clear, but the cash issue meant that the company was about to close down.

XY knew that the payment problems from the customer were due to administrative and management issues and not that the company was in financial trouble. This fact was important, as that, if the customer seemed to have been in financial trouble, then an aggressive approach should have been taken immediately before other suppliers in the same situation would have taken away all the available cash (such as employing debt collectors, etc). But, this was not the case. Furthermore, the monthly sales figures of XY's products from the customer's stores were very good, which meant that, once the customer sort out their payment problems, the opportunity should still be there for XY to capitalise on.

On the other hand, XY found itself in a catch 22, being unable to pay their own suppliers, and couldn't grow the business as previously planned due to the cash shortage. All of this while the banks were counting interest on the borrowed money as well, eating away from the company's bottom line.

When faced with such a dilemma, it is super difficult and stressful, and affects everything and everyone in the business. Relationships between the business partners (if they are more than one) becomes very difficult as each approaches this differently, and opinions may be quite extreme. Personal lives feel the strain because, let's face it, the first person who doesn't get paid when the company doesn't have enough cash is the business owner, which means big struggles on the family front as well, while probably working three times as much and as hard as usual to try and get out of the tough situation.

The reduction in stock replenishment means a sudden drop in sales, so revenue figures also drop significantly due to this, meaning that the company will continue to have further cash issues even after getting paid from that first customer.

A rather grim picture, you have to admit...

### *AB Company (selling services)*
A consulting company we worked closely with (we'll call it AB) had a decent portfolio of customers across three continents. Business was booming, and things were going rather well. All consultants were busy on highly paying jobs, and things seemed to have been going really well. Well, this was until the company's financials were looked at. You see, the company did not have proper financial controls in place, and the company's shareholders/directors were the main consultants. They thought they would have the time to do their jobs as well as do the company accounts and follow what they were doing. As things were going well, they did not notice that things were actually much worse than anyone would have thought.

AB prided themselves to always be overdelivering, and this came at a cost hidden from them until it hit them in the face. Customers would pay them for specific projects, which were previously agreed in full. The consultants would then go off and start working on the jobs, but they always ended up facing some extra work, whether in additional work they did not initially account for in their proposal, underestimating time spent to fulfil the project, underestimating costs, or even underestimating travel costs for the lead consultants on the project, whom had to do jobs for customers in different countries at the same time.

The first main item appearing to have gone out of control was travel. Some of the staff had to take over 50 flights per year (an average of one flight per week), with the additional costs of accommodation, board, transportation, etc. Since traveling from one client's country to another's was not accounted for in either client's fees, those expenses added up to significant amounts that ate up all what was left from any fees the company made.

Moreover, the additional work not accounted for in the proposals or the calculation of the fees meant that consultants ended up overworked and underpaid, as well as the company not getting paid the fair amount to cover the actual work done.

It would be very easy for someone looking from the outside into the company to say that AB were stupid not to see it, but when you are actually

# Learn From The Failures Of Others - Cashflow Will Kill Your Business

inside the work, and if you are especially overworked, you, as the entrepreneur, usually do not have the luxury of time to sit down and analyse and adjust. And, when your figures are not up to date (for whatever reason), you really end up sailing without a compass until you either get that compass reading and avoid collision or end up crashing into the rocks.

# CHAPTER III

## *How To Avoid (Start-up)*

For a new company which doesn't yet have an established base of customers and the cash flow is still right, this needs to be planned before starting. The business plan needs to have contingencies for all those eventualities, since Murphy's Law applies in a rather big way when it comes to business. Whatever problem you don't plan for WILL happen; guaranteed!

Cash for all outgoings, and not just overheads, needs to be planned from "non-customer" sources for at least 6 months to a year. And when we say all outgoings, we mean ALL outgoings! Planning the cash flow for this period can be the difference between the new business going strong in 10 years or going bankrupt within 2-3 years from starting. If you, as a start-up entrepreneur, are going to focus on nothing else, this should be your number 1 priority in the planning phase.

The cash requirements and needs don't have to be actual cash in the bank. This can also be credit facilities, such as directors loans, overdrafts or credit cards, although this is another minefield that you need to approach with extreme caution. We talk about debt in more detail in another part of this series.

So, in addition to the initial investment, you need to know exactly how much you will be able to get in credit facilities from your bank (such as overdraft), the possibility of short-term loans, what credit limit you will get on your new company credit card, etc. Add to that a commitment from the business partners to provide loans to the company in case there is a cash shortage, but this needs to be very clear from the start as to how much each may be paying and what this cash would cover if it is needed.

Adding all the above should bring you to the figure of how much cash your new company will have available. If the total amount is not enough to cover at least 6 months to one full year of overheads AND inventory (if you are selling products), then you need to either find additional sources of funding or reduce your expenses until the two figures balance. Even better is a case where the available cash is more than your needs for the first year,

# Learn From The Failures Of Others - Cashflow Will Kill Your Business

so that you have a buffer for any unforeseen eventualities or sudden expansions needing the cash.

If the total cash available is less than your outgoings for 6 months to one year and you go ahead and start the business, expect the business to fail very quickly and painfully! This is the harsh reality and we won't try and make it sound any less dangerous than it actually is!

Just go back to your plan, to your partners, to your banks, and make your calculations again accordingly. We cannot emphasise enough the importance of this step in your planning process!

The second most important element in your planning to avoid this cash problem is your terms of sales. You probably already have your price list ready and looking good, but you cannot start sending it to potential customers without the proper terms and conditions in place. Your terms have to clearly state what happens in cases of late payment, and you may even include some early payment discounts to make sure you get paid early, if possible.

Always remember that every day your customer is late paying you, this means that you are financing their business. This becomes very unfair if you are just a small start-up and they are big and established, as really there is no reason why you should be financing a giant and you struggling. We see this more and more with service companies, where they end up doing much more than their actual job entails, their costs overrunning, and not getting paid on time. Avoid this at all costs by making sure your payment terms and conditions are clear and strictly follow them! Do not compromise on that one.

If you're in a service industry, always assume that whatever you anticipate the work to be, you will always do at least 10-15% more than you think, hence your cost calculations (and your fees) have to have 10-15% buffer built into them.

If you sell products, it is always better to run out of stock than to sit on stock for months and not shifting it. Therefore, always negotiate with your suppliers that you'll buy less than your anticipated needs and have them ready to ship last minute if you need more. Do not lock your cash in inventory that won't sell, even if this means that you end up paying slightly more for the product initially.

And, whatever industry you're in, alway assume that your customers will be late paying you. ALWAYS! Then plan accordingly.

Finally, once you start negotiating with customers, do not give away too much. Buyers will always want to squeeze the last drop of money out of you and will try to negotiate the longest payment terms possible. Go into these negotiations prepared by knowing exactly what your industry norms are for payment terms, and be creative as to how you could potentially make those terms be in your favour while still appealing to the customer.

What we have found to work for larger customers, such as the early payment discounts, do not necessarily work for the smaller customers, who may be more interested in getting additional services or further discounts on their products if they reach a certain threshold, but they would always stretch the payment date as far as possible.

Spend as much time as you can doing your homework, always thinking about how you will get cash in as quickly as possible, and what you will do in the case of not receiving payments on time. And, we have to say it again, always make sure that you have enough cash to cover ALL your expenses for a full year!

Learn From The Failures Of Others - Cashflow Will Kill Your Business

# CHAPTER IV

## *How To Deal With The Problem (Established Business)*

For a business that has been established for a while that faces such hurdles, this problem can be much more difficult to deal with, since you are actually in it already. You are already going through the stressful time of suppliers chasing you, you're late paying bills, you are probably not being paid yourself, you can't cover the growth of sales or even maintaining current sales levels, and things seem to be spiralling out of control.

But, you would hope that by now you will have established some kind of strong relationship with your most important suppliers, and you can then talk with them honestly about the situation and they will hopefully help by being patient. Being honest and open about the reasons behind the cash shortage will go a long way with your suppliers, and, if they can be patient, they will be. Remember the example above of XY company and how they dealt with their late paying customer, just because they saw that the delay was not intentional. Yet you have to remember, they'll have the same issues as you if you are late paying, which is a position you don't want to be the cause of.

As an established business that is facing this problem, there are certain realities which need to be faced before any further steps are taken. First, you have to accept that the company will have to get smaller in size before being able to recover. This reduction in size might be a reduction in sales, reduction in operations, etc. Whatever it is, it will be a reduction proportional to how deep the problem goes.

Second, this reduction in size will go on for some time, so patience and being level-headed are a crucial part of the recovery process. How calm you are in this phase will be what gets you out of this situation. So, however difficult things are, and whatever noise you are hearing around you, you have to stay very calm, do not react to anything, and make rational thinking your best friend (as it will probably be your only friend by now until you turn things around).

Third, you have to accept the fact that there are people who will be

# Learn From The Failures Of Others - Cashflow Will Kill Your Business

upset with you. For whatever reason, whether at work or at home, when you get into such financial troubles, there will be people who get upset with you. Your business partners/investors may blame you for the situation, if you have to lay off staff they will be upset, your suppliers who are not being paid on time are not going to be impressed, etc. Just stay calm. This is all expected, and, once you get out of this situation, things will change and you can all become friends again. Your priority now is to get the business back up and running, and it is not to win any popularity contest.

Once you have accepted these above facts, you can now start to face the reality of the situation and try to sort it out.

1. When it comes to cash problems, the first thing you need to do is to stop any cash going out that is unnecessary. By saying "unnecessary" we mean EVERYTHING that, if you get rid of it today, the company is still functioning. This may be magazine subscriptions, certain additional benefits you provide staff with, company vehicles, large offices, travel of all sorts, and even staff. If you are currently working from an office, try to either downsize or even get rid of the office completely and have as many people as possible work from home. If you have a large warehouse, start to downsize it, put more stock that you already have in your warehouse at customers' stores with the best potential for sales and the best potential of getting paid on time, and just get the smallest warehousing facility possible to cut that expense.

    When it comes to deciding on which staff to keep and which to let go, you have to really look at every role and see if one person can do two or three jobs instead of having three people do it. This usually means it is you, the entrepreneur, who will end up doing a lot of the work, but at least you are not draining more money until you recover. Once you recover, you can hire people again to do those jobs (and we are sure you'll be better at judging how many people to hire and their cost).

    You are going to lose money when taking this step. It is inevitable. You are going to lose money on selling vehicles, getting out of your rent contracts, paying redundancies, etc. But, always remember that you are now at a stage where the bottom line means nothing until you have some cash back in your hand! And, anything that will take cash from you in a week or a month from now has to go at any cost! YOUR ONLY FOCUS NOW IS CASH AND STOPPING THE BLEEDING! NOTHING ELSE!

2. The second step to take is to start to try and collect any cash at all that is out there, even if it is not late! Sometimes, companies in a difficult cash situation would find not having cash just for one day makes a huge

difference. So, every day your priority is to get cash in from every possible direction. One way of doing this is to offer an "early payment discount" to customers who are not late paying but still have a few more weeks until their payments become due. Your relationship with your customers will play a major role in this, as you try and get those with a good relationship with you to pay early even without that haircut.

3. You have now stopped the ongoing bleeding, and you have put a bandage on it by getting whatever cash is outside, so you need to start treating the actual cashflow issue to move forward. You need to start working on getting in new sales without having to put out more cash.

### *SERVICE COMPANY?*
If you are selling services, try to add some services to your existing customers. We know that this sounds like we are telling you that you have to do something you are already doing, but we have seen it time and again that businesses lose focus and turn their attention to trying to get new customers in, which takes more effort and money and they still have the risk of not getting the business. Turning your attention to your existing customers means that you have to sit down and think about how you can improve their lives in any way possible. Provide them with something that they would be grateful for, even if it is not paid now. The additional service you provide them with will mean that they should turn to you the next time they want to buy the service, or they wouldn't say no to you when you suggest to sell them another service or renew your agreement.

### *SELLING PRODUCTS?*
If you are selling products, start off by trying to get rid of ALL the inventory you still have. Just get rid of it at any cost. Ideally, you will be able to make a little bit of money on it, but be prepared to sell it at cost or even at a small loss. Remember that your priority now is to have cash in your hand in order to be able to survive.

Talk to your suppliers while you are in this process. Sometimes suppliers might be able to match some demands from other companies wanting to buy stock which you have, or they might even help out by buying back some of your stock themselves if they are running low (or just to help you out). Just focus on the fastest way to empty your warehouse asap!

4. You're now ready to change the way you do business to get back on track. Now that you have cut out all the fat, bandaged the wounds and

# Learn From The Failures Of Others - Cashflow Will Kill Your Business

got into a relatively stable position, take the next step into getting your business back and start to get some money in. At this stage, you might have to deviate a little from your original plans of how your business runs or its main operational focus, and all operations have to revolve around the best way to make cash quickly and not get in the red. All you sales, without exception, have to be making money AND you have to get cash in quickly BEFORE any cash goes out.

This phase has to go on until your business starts to get back on track. Getting back on track means that you will have paid off all your outstanding amounts and you have regular steady stream of cash coming in to comfortably cover your overheads.

5. The final stage will be to get your business back to follow the original plan, albeit with some adjustments to how you and everyone else in the company do things. To go back to the original plan will have you treat your business as a new start-up, where you have enough of a cash cushion to lean on for quite some time until the wheels start to move again at full speed. You just need to follow the steps mentioned in the previous chapter, which outline how a start-up business can avoid falling into the cash shortage trap.

Round Square Ventures Ltd

# CHAPTER V

## *Summary Of Solutions*

So, what's the summary of this?

Cash shortage can kill your business, and it can be completely out of your hands how this comes along. The start-up entrepreneur should always focus on this thoroughly in the planning process, and an established company that is currently facing this problem should focus all their efforts to stopping the bleeding to be able to recover.

**Avoiding this as a start-up:**

- Never ever assume that the business will cover its own cash-flow needs in the first year or two.
- All expenses for the first 6-12 months have to be 100% covered by cash that is not dependent on revenues. Expenses include everything, even inventory for the full period.
- You need to make sure that you have enough short-term credit facilities to cover your cash needs if you face a cash shortage.
- Do not start to send out prices to customers until your terms of sales are prepared, and be prepared yourself to strictly follow them.
- If you sell services, always assume that your costs will be 10-15% more than you think, and include this in your cost forecasts and your fee calculations.
- If you sell products, always try to buy less inventory than you need and try to agree with your suppliers to send more at short notice. Remember, it is better to run out of inventory than sit on inventory that doesn't sell.
- Always assume that customer will be late paying you, and plan accordingly.
- Give customers incentives to pay you early. There is no one size that fits all here, so you need to adapt to each customer to ensure you get paid on time or early. Early payment discounts, additional services or bonus

## Learn From The Failures Of Others - Cashflow Will Kill Your Business

products are all ways to incentivise customers to pay early.
- Take your time doing your homework to understand the market and your customers, and always think of how you can get paid quickly and early.

**For an established business**, this can be trickier.
- Start off by being honest and open with your suppliers to try and fix the situation of you delaying payments to them.
- Stop ALL unnecessary expenses. Downsize facilities, staff, vehicles, memberships, etc. even if it means you're going to lose some money in this process. You want to cut "ongoing" expenses.
- Start to collect anything you have outstanding, even if it hasn't become due yet. Give incentives to customers to pay you early, and do not forget the late paying customers either in your collection rounds! You just want cash in as quickly as possible.
- If you sell services, start offering additional services to your customers to get more out of them at a discounted rate, making sure they pay early.
- If you sell products, your goal will be to clear any inventory you still have, even if it means losing some money on it. You just want the cash!
- Once the above is done, start to approach your business in a different way to generate cash as quickly as possible, making sure that no expenses are paid before the cash comes in. This means that you might have to deviate from original plans for a while.
- Once you're out of trouble, you need to look at the plans again and treat your business as a start-up. To avoid the cashflow issues, follow the steps in the "start-up" solutions.

We know this is by no means an exhaustive list, but we hope it gets you thinking about your business cash needs in a way to help either avoid the problems of cash shortage or help you with some ideas to recover from it if you've already fallen into it.

If you found this short book useful, share it with your friends so that they can make use of the information in it.

And, be on the look out for other short books in this series for more business mistakes and how you can avoid them and/or correct them.

Good luck!

Round Square Ventures Ltd

# ABOUT THE AUTHORS

Round Square Ventures Ltd is a company that specialises in business consulting and operation management in Europe, North America and the Middle East. The company's founders have been starting and running businesses since the early 1990s, with a vast experience across several industries.

RSV have helped start and run companies of all sizes, from small one-person working from home entities, to trans-national multi-million dollar conglomerates.

The team of consultants and managers at RSV have actually been running their own businesses within the industries they focus on, so they don't just follow theoretical lines, but also draw on their own experiences.

The RSV team bring their collective experiences into writing books with the goal of helping new entrepreneurs kick-start their adventure into the business world, or assist established business people in their quest for growth and/or recovery.

www.ingramcontent.com/pod-product-compliance
Lightning Source LLC
Chambersburg PA
CBHW070847220526
45466CB00002B/913